The Old West may be gone, but memories and legend live on.

Ask any cowpoke and, boy howdy, he'll tell some tales. Ask a cowboy from Umatilla County, and he'll for sure come around to the story of the Saddle Bronc Championship at the 1911 Pendleton Round-Up—and a bronc buster named **George Fletcher.** George was a rider folks in those parts can never forget. Even made it into the National Cowboy Hall of Fame. But we're puttin' the wagon ahead of the horse. **We gotta go back a ways to reckon how he got there. Tell you what, it wasn't easy.**

For the Nelsons and the Helweges,
true westerners who embody the cowboy spirit

and

For my pards, the dandy Snyders
—V.M.N.

To my parents for all of their love, patience, and support
—G.C.J.

Text copyright © 2019 by Vaunda Micheaux Nelson
Illustrations copyright © 2019 by Gordon C. James

The phrase "Let 'Er Buck" is trademarked by the Pendleton Round-Up Association and is used with permission.

Carolrhoda Books
A division of Lerner Publishing Group, Inc.
241 First Avenue North
Minneapolis, MN 55401 USA

For reading levels and more information, look up this title at www.lernerbooks.com.

Photos courtesy of the Umatilla County Historical Society.

Design by Danielle Carnito.
Main body text set in Imperfect OT 14.5/19.5. Typeface provided by T26.
The illustrations in this book were created with oil on board.

Library of Congress Cataloging-in-Publication Data

Names: Nelson, Vaunda Micheaux, author. | James, Gordon C., illustrator.
Title: Let 'er buck! : George Fletcher, the people's champion / Vaunda Micheaux Nelson ; illustrated by Gordon C. James.
Description: Minneapolis, MN : Carolrhoda Books, 2019. | Includes bibliographical references. | Audience: 008–012.
Identifiers: LCCN 2018021311 (print) | LCCN 2018030744 (ebook) | ISBN 9781541541801 (eb pdf) | ISBN 9781512498080 (lb: alk. paper)
Subjects: LCSH: Fletcher, George, 1890–1973. | African American cowboys—Biography—Juvenile literature. | Rodeos—United States—History—Juvenile literature. | LCGFT: Biographies.
Classification: LCC GV1833.6.F54 (ebook) | LCC GV1833.6.F54 N45 2019 (print) | DDC 791.8/4092 [B]—dc23

LC record available at https://lccn.loc.gov/2018021311

Manufactured in the United States of America
1-43576-33357-7/30/2018

LET 'ER BUCK!

George
Fletcher,
the **People's
Champion**

VAUNDA MICHEAUX NELSON
illustrated by GORDON C. JAMES

Carolrhoda Books
Minneapolis

George had to buck up and get tough at an early age.

He was just about ten years old around the turn of the century when his family packed up and lit out from Kansas on the Oregon Trail.

They had folks in Pendleton, so it seemed as good a settling place as any. But there weren't many black people in Eastern Oregon, and most whites in Pendleton didn't cotton to them. George suffered meanness and hurt because of his skin color. Life at home was no bushel of peaches either. He had to make his own way.

George found a kinship with the children he'd come to know from the Umatilla Indian Reservation, where members of the Walla Walla, the Cayuse, and the Umatilla tribes lived. George was so good-natured they found him easy to like back. He started bunking with the families of his Indian friends. George took to their ways like a wet kitten to a warm brick. As they played together, he learned their languages and how they saw the world.

George's favorite game was riding a make-believe bronco.

One boy straddled a barrel while others pulled cables attached to make it "buck." George wrapped his legs tight around the imaginary horse and clenched his knees. It was plain as the ears on a mule he was born to ride.

George was purely tickled when he moved up to riding beef calves. But when his hip pockets first landed on a horse, he was smitten. He got thrown a lot at first but just kept getting back on. Every day George marveled more at these magnificent animals. He was spellbound by the drumming of hooves beneath him, the swirling and swaying, the rocking and reeling—his dance with a wild mustang. This was where he belonged.

George watched the tribal horsemen and listened well. From them he learned to train horses in a calm and gentle way. He never pushed. Took it slow, talking soft, touching easy all over, gaining trust. He blew lightly into their nostrils so they could breathe him in. With his tender manner, George could tame a horse without breaking what he loved so much—its spirit.

Ranching fit George like made-to-measure boots. Life in the saddle and riding rough were all he hankered for. George knew he could ride just about anything. He first rode for prizes at the age of sixteen, but some rodeos and exhibitions shut out black cowboys. When he *was* allowed to compete, the judges hardly ever treated him fair. It stung, but that didn't stop George. He was set on showing what he was made of.

At one Wild West show, George offered to ride the worst of the worst in a saddle bronc contest. Handlers tried to ruin his ride by turning the horse loose before George was up and ready, but George showed them a thing or two. He swung into the saddle, rode the animal to a standstill, and won the day.

In farm rodeos and staged exhibitions around Pendleton, George rode horses, bulls, even buffalo. If it bucked, he was getting aboard. One time, George and another black cowboy named Jesse Stahl gave spectators a show to beat all. They rode the same bucking bronco seated back to back, with George facing the animal's head and Jesse facing south.

Folks liked putting George to the test, challenging him to ride the most ill-tempered beasts just to see if he could.

One day he took a dare and mounted a bad bronc on a city street in downtown Pendleton. He rode the buck out of the bruiser but got himself arrested because their dance spilled up onto the sidewalk. George faced a judge and paid the five-dollar fine, still eager to show off his skill. He got his chance a few months later at the 1911 Pendleton Round-Up.

It was the biggest rodeo in the Northwest. Fifteen thousand fired-up fans packed the grandstand. Horse racing, bull riding, steer wrestling, roping, and other tests of cowboy skill, nerve, and vigor brought cheers and groans from onlookers. But nothing beat the Saddle Bronc Championship. Three top-notch buckaroos made the finals:

Jackson Sundown,
a Nez Perce Indian,

John Spain,
a white rancher,

and twenty-one-year-old
George Fletcher.

The prize was a $350
silver-trimmed Hamley saddle.

The broncs were about half wild.

Local stockmen brought their roughest, most unrideable "outlaws" to the event. Luck of the draw matched them up with riders. Each cowboy pulled a horse's name from a hat, hoping for a rank, hard-bucking cayuse. Half the winning points came from the horse. The tougher the outlaw, the higher the score.

A buckaroo choked the reins with one hand and kept his other in the air. Any cowboy who "pulled leather"—touched the saddle or horse with his free hand—was disqualified. Bronc busters stayed on as long as they could or till the animal bucked out.

First up was Jackson Sundown, riding Lightfoot.

Jackson was forty-eight years old, but didn't look it—far from it. He was tall, lean, handsome. Carried himself with smooth elegance. Like George, Jackson had been rough riding since boyhood and had earned his reputation as a horseman.

Lightfoot was fierce and furious. He leaped and twisted, snorted and kicked, even turned and tried to bite Jackson's leg. Jackson, his long braids flying, kept his seat until Lightfoot turned tricky and charged into one of the mounted judges. Saddle crashed against saddle, and Jackson's foot wrenched free. He took flight and kissed the ground. Sundown was carried off on a stretcher but was hurt most by being disqualified for losing a stirrup.

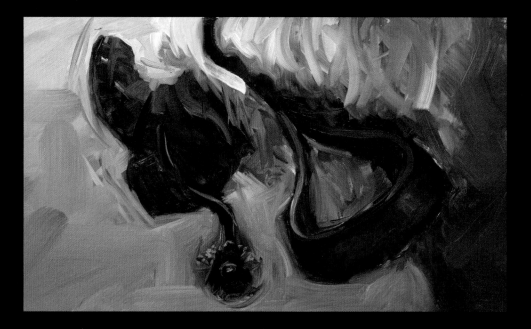

John Spain rode next, forking Long Tom.

John was thirty years old, six feet of rock solid. He stuck to bucking horses by sheer muscle and grit. Inspired at an early age by Buffalo Bill's Wild West, he'd been riding the shows half his life.

Long Tom was brawny and athletic. An expert bucker, he easily threw most riders. John wasn't most riders. Tom lunged and plunged, pitched and heaved. In a final effort, the outlaw crashed through a wooden fence between the arena and the racetrack. It was a dandy ride, but onlookers claimed Spain pulled leather when Tom broke through the barrier. The judges said they hadn't seen it.

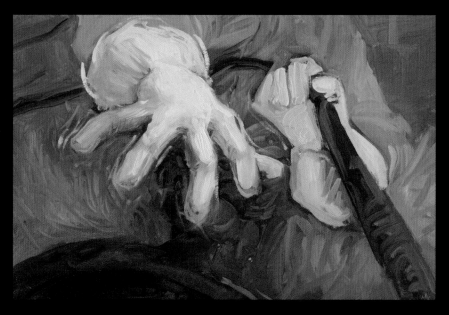

At last it was George's turn.

Shouts of **"Let 'er buck,"** cascaded from the stands. George had earned the esteem of the crowd with a sensational semifinal ride on Hot Foot—a mean, jackknifing piece of horseflesh.

George tipped his hat to the crowd and mounted Del. He was ready, but the horse wasn't. Usually a prime performer, Del dipped, tossed, and ran but, doggone it, the obstinate outlaw refused to buck. It looked like George's luck had soured.

"Re-ride!" the crowd clamored.

"Re-ride! Re-ride!"

The judges chewed on this awhile. Then one spoke through the megaphone, **"Saddle another for Fletcher!"**

Handlers led Sweeney into the arena.

Sweeney was a high-jumping, sunfishing, arm jerker. He reared on his hind legs and bucked wildly.

Unfazed, George quickly found the rhythm of the ride, the rise and fall, the whirl and twirl, the spin and swerve of outlaw and horseman.

Calls rang out, **"Ride 'im, George! Ride 'im!"** George stayed with Sweeney, raking his spurs from shoulder to flank. Even waved his hat and smiled. Fans leapt to their boots—cheering and howling,

"Let 'er buck! Let 'er buck!"

George "rode Sweeney with SUCH EASE AND ABANDON that the crowd shouted itself hoarse." He was "as LIMBER AND ELASTIC as a rubber band" and "easily made the MOST SHOWY RIDE" of the Round-Up.

That's how the newspaper told it.

➤———

After the ride, everybody stood rapt, waiting for the winner to be announced. In due time, one of the judges called through the megaphone,

"John Spain, first. George Fletcher, second."

Silence filled the arena.

"Boo! Boo!" erupted from the stands. Spectators were certain George would be the champion. The crowd roared angrily, but the judges' decision was final. George took it like a cowboy. He'd felt this sting before.

John Spain, astride the prize Hamley saddle, made his victory ride past the grandstand as the crowd applauded.

When George Fletcher loped by on his old, worn saddle, fans exploded with unbridled cries and whistles.

Sheriff Tillman Taylor was a Round-Up board member and a man of honor. This didn't sit right with him.

The Umatilla County lawman plucked the hat from George's head and cut it into small pieces with a jackknife. He waved a piece in the air. Rodeo goers caught on fast and eagerly paid five dollars each for a George Fletcher keepsake. When all was said and done, those folks collected more money for George than the price of the silver-trimmed prize saddle. They'd plumb decided—heck with the judges—George'd won.

In the warm glow of the setting sun, spirited spectators lifted George onto their shoulders and paraded around the arena. Someone hollered, **"People's Champion,"** which swelled to a resounding, united chorus—**"People's Champion!**

People's Champion!

People's Champion!"

Just you ask any
Umatilla County
cowboy . . .
He'll tell you.

Rodeo and Western Words

arm jerker: a stout, athletic animal that bucks with a lot of power

boy howdy: an exclamation of excited agreement or surprise

bronc: a wild or untamed horse, from the Spanish word *bronco* meaning "rough or rude"

bruiser: a strong, husky animal or person

buckaroo: a cowboy who does ranch work for a living, from the Spanish word *vaquero*

bucker: a horse that bucks

cayuse: a cowboy term for horse. Also an Indian pony, named after the Cayuse tribe of Indians

cowpoke: cowboy

didn't cotton to: didn't like

forking: straddling a horse

Hamley: refers to the historic Pendleton, Oregon, saddlemaker Hamley & Co.

hankered for: desired, or longed for

jackknifing: when a bucking horse brings its front and rear feet together as it leaps

let 'er buck!: "Bring on the bronco and let it buck" or "bring on the challenge." It can also mean "buck up," "deal with it!" or "get on with it." It's the slogan for the Pendleton Round-Up.

lope: to move or run with long, easy strides

mustang: a small, hardy, wild horse of the western plains, directly descended from horses the Spaniards brought to the Americas

outlaw: a fierce, untamed horse, sometimes called a bad one

piece of horseflesh: horse

plumb: downright, absolutely

raking: when a rider runs the rowels of his spurs along the horse's sides. This increases the score in saddle bronc contests. A rowel is the circular, notched, free-moving part of a spur. The rowels in rodeo are blunt rather than sharp.

rank: extremely hard to ride, mean, untamed

riding the shows: competing for prize money at rodeos

rodeo: a contest of cowboy riding and roping skills, originally started as informal competitions between ranches

rough riding: riding untamed stock that bucks

rough stock: untamed ranch animals such as horses and cattle, also called bucking stock

smitten: in love, under a spell, enthralled with

spur: a device strapped to a rider's boot heel and pressed into a horse's sides to urge it to go

steer wrestling: a rodeo event in which the cowboy leaps from a running horse, grabs a steer's horns, and attempts to bring the animal to the ground; also known as bulldogging

stirrup: the part of a saddle that holds a rider's foot

sunfishing: when a bucking horse twists itself from side to side as it leaps

to beat all: an exclamation of amazement, as in, "If that don't beat all!"

George Fletcher

George's talent and commitment to his sport inspired an entire stadium of people to stand up for justice; he didn't win the saddle—he won their hearts and minds.

George Albert Fletcher was born in St. Marys, Kansas, on October 3, 1890. George's early years are not well documented, but sources suggest his family life was less than happy. Despite this, he was known for his good nature and free spirit. He managed to maintain this attitude, even though he was regularly called a variety of degrading names by Pendleton residents—the Negro boy, Pendleton's colored boy, and sometimes worse.

In the years that followed the 1911 Pendleton Round-Up, George continued to take part in it and other rodeos, fairs, and exhibitions for fun and money. Although he never was the Round-Up Saddle Bronc Champion, George won or placed in other events such as the wild horse race, cowpony race, and maverick race.

In 1918 he enlisted in the army and joined other African Americans in a Services of Supply unit during World War I. George was deployed to France where, because of his ranching and rodeo background, he was assigned to care for army horses and mules. While there, he impressed servicemen and French citizens alike with exhibition rides. During one such ride, George hurt his right leg, returning from the war in 1919 with an injury that essentially ended his days as a competitive bronc buster. Still, he participated in the Pendleton Round-Up on and

off until 1926. George spent the rest of his life working as a ranch cowboy in the Umatilla County area.

He wasn't awarded the title he earned. Yet to this day, George Fletcher is still remembered as the People's Champion and rightful saddle bronc winner of the 1911 Pendleton Round-Up.

"To George, it wasn't about being first but about being accepted as a human being, changing people's opinion of him," said Cedric Wildbill who, as a child growing up on the Umatilla Indian Reservation became friends with the aging George. "For that brief moment he could be his own man, respected for himself, for his abilities. Going in, you have a little hope, but you know you're not likely to win. But he won the crowd that day. He was victorious in the end despite not winning the judges."

In 2014 the City of Pendleton erected a bronze statue of George on Main Street.

Cedric commented, "If George Fletcher was alive today, he'd laugh and say, 'Really? They put a statue of me on Main Street?' You see, George didn't see himself as a hero." But lots of people surely did. George Fletcher was inducted into the Pendleton Round-Up and Happy Canyon Hall of Fame in 1969, the National Cowboy and Western Heritage Museum Hall of Fame in 2001 and the National Cowboys of Color Museum and Hall of Fame in 2006. He died in a nursing home on October 1, 1973, and is buried in Olney Cemetery in Pendleton.

About the Research

I have been unable to verify certain facts regarding George Fletcher's life, particularly during his early years. There is no doubt that he lived, at times, at the Umatilla Indian Reservation, home to the Umatilla, the Walla Walla, and the Cayuse tribes. How he came to be there is unclear. Some sources say young George attended the Umatilla Indian Agency Boarding School on the reservation and worked at the Tutuilla Presbyterian Church, where he was tutored and looked after by the Reverend James Cornelison. I was unable to find school enrollment or church records to support this. Other sources suggest Indians found a teenage George near death on the reservation. It's said they cared for him and welcomed him into their lives.

Conflicting information surrounds the horses George rode in the 1911 finals. All seem to agree that the first horse (which would not buck) was Del. Some sources say the re-ride was aboard Hot Foot, but others say it was on Sweeney with Hot Foot identified as the horse George rode in the semifinals. The *Pendleton East Oregonian* newspaper and Pendleton Round-Up records support the latter.

Yet another mystery involves his participation in the 1910 Pendleton Round-Up. The printed program for the Round-Up confirms George entered several events including the saddle bronc contest. The *Pendleton East Oregonian* reported results from the first day stating George placed third in the wild horse race and fourth in the cowpony race, and that George and another black cowboy, Lewis Mosely, qualified for the saddle bronc finals. Oddly, there is no mention of either man in subsequent days.

Some sources say George didn't participate in the 1910 bucking contest because he was in jail for riding a wild horse down Main Street. I could find no court record or newspaper account of George's arrest during the week of the 1910 Round-Up. I did find a newspaper report from 1907 in which sixteen-year-old George rode a bucking horse down Main Street filled with folks leaving church. A judge fined him five dollars and told him to mend his "bronco twisting ways." The incident in my story occurred in June of 1911, months before that year's Round-Up. Even if George had been in jail during the 1910 Round-Up, this wouldn't explain why Lewis Mosley's final performance wasn't reported. Although Oregon was never a slave state, its constitution and public policies at the turn of the century made it clear that blacks were not welcome.

Jackson Sundown

Jackson Sundown was born into the Wallowa band of the Nez Perce tribe in Montana about 1863. His father was Nez Perce, and his mother was Flathead. A nephew of the renowned Chief Joseph, Jackson lived in Montana, Canada and, ultimately, Idaho. He called himself Buffalo Jackson in his Montana youth when he rode bison but later adopted "Jackson Sundown." His Indian name was Waaya-Tonah-Toesits-Kahn, which means "Earth Left by the Setting Sun" or "Blanket of the Sun."

Jackson learned horsemanship from Nez Perce buffalo hunters and warriors. His skills were honed during the Nez Perce War of 1877. The US Calvary relentlessly pursued his people over 1,600 miles (2,575 km) as Chief Joseph led their flight toward Canada. Just fourteen years old, Jackson cared for the horses and assisted many who needed help. With woman and children in freezing conditions and no food or blankets, Chief Joseph had no choice but to surrender near the Canadian border on October 4, 1877. Jackson escaped to Canada and, after two years, returned to the United States.

Jackson Sundown earned a reputation as a first-rate horseman and later went on to participate in rodeos

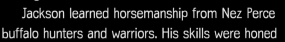

and Wild West shows in Idaho. Sometimes top riders refused to compete against him, saying Sundown would win everything. In some of these instances, Jackson was offered and accepted payment for exhibition rides instead. To demonstrate his skill and control, he sometimes would insert a coin under his boot in each stirrup. After riding a bucking horse, the coins would still be there.

After the 1911 contest, he became a regular in the Pendleton Round-Up and was known for excellent riding as well as dynamic showmanship. Sundown had a winning smile and wore brightly colored scarves, shirts, and shaggy angora chaps. Before competing, he tied his braids together in the front under his neckerchief, but they sometimes jerked free during the ride. He qualified for the finals in the Round-Up bucking contest for five consecutive years after 1911 and placed third in 1915. Finally, his banner year came in 1916 when, at the age of

fifty-three, Sundown won the Pendleton Round-Up Saddle Bronc Championship and a $500 Hamley saddle. He was more than twice the age of his two competitors in the finals. Years later, old cowboys recalled Jackson's 1916 saddle bronc ride on Angel as the best they'd ever seen. He was also awarded the coveted All-Round Cowboy title that year. Jackson never competed in another Round-Up after 1916 but faithfully returned to watch and reminisce. He worked as a rancher and horse trainer for the rest of his life.

Jackson Sundown died on December 18, 1923, and he is buried at Slickpoo Cemetery in northwest Idaho. He was inducted into the Pendleton Round-Up and Happy Canyon Hall of Fame in 1972 and the National Cowboy and Western Heritage Museum Hall of Fame in 1976. A bronze statue of Jackson was erected on Pendleton's Main Street in 2013.

John Spain

John Spain was born in Cottage Grove, Oregon, October 10, 1881, and spent his early childhood growing up in Union, Oregon. To escape problems at home, he and his older brother Fred left as young boys (eleven and nine) and became inseparable. They went on to become committed ranchers. After seeing Buffalo Bill's Wild West, the Spain brothers began staging their own shows in northwestern Oregon. They also provided rough stock to rodeos in the

JOHN SPAINE ON LONG TOM WINNING CHAMPIONSHIP OF THE NORTHWEST BUCKING CONTEST 1911.

been fair. "The judges said so, at least, and their word must go. Fletcher made a good ride all the way through. If he made a better ride than I, the judges should have given him the saddle. There is no trouble or argument between George Fletcher and me." George told the *Pendleon Live Wire* that Spain had "pulled leather" and "the drawing of the color line" was the deciding factor. The judges said John had better form and had ridden a more challenging horse.

area. In 1909 they received a letter from Sheriff Tillman Taylor, livestock director of the Pendleton Round-Up, asking them to supply horses for the first Round-Up. John and Fred also had the honor of leading the Westward Ho! Parade at the first Pendleton Round-Up in 1910.

About the controversial 1911 championship, John told the *Pendleton Live Wire* newspaper that the win had

One year later, at a 1912 Independence Day rodeo, John lost his right hand in a roping accident. Most thought his rodeo career was over, but John wouldn't have it. He continued to compete and win. John Spain died on December 8, 1928, and is buried at Mt. Hope Cemetery in Baker City, Oregon. He was inducted into the Pendleton Round-Up and Happy Canyon Hall of Fame in 2011.

Sheriff Tillman Taylor

At the age of three, Tillman D. Taylor came to Umatilla County with his pioneer parents. Born near Silverton, Oregon, on September 19, 1866, he dedicated his life to bringing peace to the county. Til was elected Umatilla County sheriff in 1902. When community officials proposed holding a frontier show and rodeo, the sheriff was supportive. He saw a need to control the good-natured rowdyism of cowboys who sometimes went too far. The idea of a Pendleton Round-Up would be a positive, orderly way to direct and release this cowpoke energy. Because Til knew many ranchers, he was made livestock director in charge of obtaining horses and steers for the first Round-Up in 1910. Sources say it was Til Taylor who invited the tribes from the Umatilla Indian Reservation to participate in the first Round-Up, which they have done ever since. He was Round-Up president from 1912 to 1920.

Til was charming, sincere, generous, and moral. He was also a shrewd and daring lawman, known for stellar skills in solving crimes and tracking down men and women who lived outside the law.

Sheriff Taylor's strong sense of justice was likely the motivation for his actions at the 1911 Round-Up. During his time as sheriff, he took an interest in George Fletcher, hiring him as a tracker and unofficial deputy. Sheriff Taylor, like the Reverend James Cornelison, hoped to provide stability for George, who occasionally found trouble or trouble found him. Although Til had great affection for his Umatilla County home, he was opposed to the antiblack sentiment that existed there and, as in George's case, let this be known.

Til served as county sheriff for eighteen years. He was shot and killed on July 25, 1920, at the Umatilla County Jail while attempting to stop a jailbreak. In 1923 Pendleton established Til Taylor Memorial Park honoring the memory of peace officers who died in the line of duty. Six years later, the city erected a statue honoring the Oregon lawman in the park bearing his name.

Bits and Pieces

When he was nineteen, George took third place in a bronc-busting contest at the 1909 Eastern Oregon District Fair. He called the fifteen-dollar prize the easiest money he ever made.

In 1918 the Round-Up contributed all of its profits to support the Red Cross during World War I. The Pendleton Round-Up has taken place every fall since 1910 except in 1942 and 1943, when it was canceled due to World War II.

All workers at the Pendleton Round-Up are volunteers. Unlike most other rodeos, there is no advertising posted in the arena.

Rules for some rodeo events have changed since 1911. Then, bronc busters stayed on the horse for as long as they could. Today a successful ride ends at eight seconds.

The $5 prize in 1911 would be equal to about $128 in 2018, making the $350 prize Hamley saddle worth $8,960.

Women competed in all events at the Round-Up until 1929 when a female died from injuries suffered in a bronc-riding accident, and the directors banned women from bucking contests. In 1990 women returned to competing in rough stock events.

One in four cowboys in the Old West were black, and even more were Mexican. Mexicans were the original cowboys, or vaqueros.

Rodeo legend Jesse Stahl was arguably one of the best bronc riders ever, but old timers remember him "winning first, but getting third" because of his race.

Selected Bibliography

Books

Adams, Ramon F. *Cowboy Lingo: A Dictionary of the Slack-Jaw Words and Whangdoodle Ways of the American West.* Boston: Houghton Mifflin, 2000.

Bales, Michael, and Ann Terry Hill. *Pendleton Round-Up at 100: Oregon's Legendary Rodeo.* Portland, OR: Graphic Arts Books, 2009.

Boylen, "Pink" E. N. *Episode of the West: The Pendleton Round-Up 1910–1951, Facts and Figures*, E. N. Boylen, 1975.

Crockatt, Ernest L. *The Murder of Til Taylor: A Great Western Sheriff.* Philadelphia: Dorrance, 1970.

Furlong, Charles Wellington. *Let 'er Buck: A Story of the Passing of the Old West.* New York: Overlook, 1921.

Gibson, Elizabeth. *Pendleton.* Charleston, SC: Arcadia, 2014.

Jordon, Bob. *Rodeo History and Legends.* Montrose, CO: Rodeo Stuff, 1994.

Porter, Willard H. *Who's Who in Rodeo.* Oklahoma City: Powder River, 1982.

Rupp, Virgil. *Let 'er Buck! A History of the Pendleton Round-Up.* Pendleton, OR: Pendleton Round-Up Association, 1985.

Steber, Rick. *Red White Black: A True Story of Race and Rodeo.* Prineville, OR: printed by the author, 2013.

Articles

"Bucking Horse on Main." *Pendleton Daily East Oregonian*, April 15, 1907.

"Colored Boy Arrested." *Pendleton Daily East Oregonian*, June 28, 1911.

Kirkpatrick, Rita. "Jackson Sundown: Nez Perce Champion Bronc Buster." *La Mesa (CA) Indian Trader*, September 1975.

"Kit Carson Show Proves to Be a Fake." *Pendleton Daily East Oregonian*, June 28, 1911.

Olson, Jim. "Jesse Stahl: First Black Bronc Rider." *Arizona in the Saddle*, July 2015, 30–31.

Patch, Charles C. "Negro Cowboy." *Real West*, October 1968, 32–33.

"Round-Up Hall of Famer Dies." *Pendleton East Oregonian*, October 3, 1973.

Soodalter, Ron. "The Unforgettable 1911 Pendleton Round-Up." *Cowboys & Indians*, October 2016, 134–141.

"When George Fletcher Rode for Bucking Championship." *Pendleton East Oregonian*, September 13, 1913.

"Young Boy Wins Saddle." *Pendleton East Oregonian*, October 1, 1909.

Videos

American Cowboys. Written, directed and produced by Cedric Wildbill and Tania Wildbill. Narrated by William Hurt. Pendleton, OR: Wildbill, 1998. DVD.

Let 'er Buck: A Time of Legends (1910–1930) A Colorful History of the Early Days of the Pendleton Round-Up. A film by Wes Houle. WH Pictures, 2008. DVD.

Interviews

Ransom, Leon, son of a friend of George Fletcher. Telephone interview with the author, April 2017.

Steber, Rick, author. Telephone interview with the author, April 2017.

Wildbill, Cedric, writer, director, producer. Interview with the author in Pendleton, OR, March 2017.

Acknowledgments

I am much obliged to researcher Virginia Roberts of Pendleton for giving so generously of her time and knowledge, to Lori Snyder for research assistance, and to Lori and her husband, Greg Snyder, for taking me on a road trip to Pendleton. Thanks to my agent Tracey Adams, my editor Carol Hinz, art director Danielle Carnito, and my publishing family at Lerner. Much gratitude to Gordon C. James for his vibrant illustrations. I'm indebted to Malissa Minthon Winks and Marjorie Waheneka of Tamástslikt Cultural Institute and Beth Piatote (associate professor Native American Studies) at the University of California, Berkeley, for their helpful review of the manuscript. Many thanks to the Pendleton Round-Up Trademark Committee—Rob Collins, Tiah DeGrofft, Jason Graybeal, and Nick Sirovatka—for their consideration and permission. A big yee-haw to librarian Nancy Oberdick of Rio Rancho Public Library, Cedric Wildbill, Tania Wildbill, Rick Steber, Michael Bales, Leon Ransom, Betty Branstetter, archivist Charliann Cross of the National Archives at Seattle, the Pendleton Round-Up and Happy Canyon Hall of Fame, Christiana Gunderson, Rebecca Struthers of the *Pendleton East Oregonian*, Executive Director Barbara Lund-Jones at Heritage Station, the Umatilla County Historical Society Museum, Steve Churchill of the Umatilla County Office of County Records, Elizabeth Peterson of the University of Oregon Libraries, Melody Rosenberg of the Pendleton Public School District, and to Pendleton Public Library. Special thanks to my writing critique group—Katherine Hauth, Stephanie Farrow, Caroline Starr Rose, and Uma Krishnaswami. I'm most beholden to my husband, Drew, for ideas, editorial and literary wisdom, friendship, and love. Above all, I thank my Lord for enabling me to continue this fulfilling work.